FABRIC OF HUMANITY

Abhijit Naskar is the twenty-first century mind of science, whose glorious philosophical touch has enabled modern Neuroscience to effectively engage in the human society towards diminishing the ever-growing conflicts among religions. As an untiring advocate of global harmony and peace, he became a beloved best-selling author all over the world with his very first book "The Art of Neuroscience in Everything". With various of his pioneering ventures into the Neuropsychology of religious sentiments, he has hugely contributed to humanity's attempt of eradicating religious differences, for which he is popularly hailed as a humanitarian who incessantly works towards taking the human civilization in the path of sweet general harmony.

FABRIC OF
HUMANITY

ABHIJIT NASKAR

Fabric of Humanity

Copyright © 2018 Abhijit Naskar

This is a work of non-fiction

An Amazon Publishing Company, 1st Edition, 2018

Printed in United States of America

ISBN: 9781729345856

DEDICATION

Shankara

CONTENTS

SONNET OF HUMAN

Sonnet of Human

I am but a human who's got no name,

Simply alive in the land of liberty,

I am but a human who talks no lame,

Simply communicates with utter serenity,

I am but a human who despises harming,

No matter what some books command,

I am but a human who loves not blaming,

No matter how much my peers demand,

I am but a human who lives not in history,

Simply breathes in the now and here,

I am but a human who's curious in mystery,

And loves to investigate forged with questionnaire,

I am but a human teeming with awareness beyond all race and clans,

I am but a human whose religion is liberty and god the humans.

BE THE HARMONY

To begin our never-ending journey of peace, first you must give me something. I want something from you my friend - and it's going to be hard to give - it is going to put extreme labor on your mind. Give me your prejudices - give me your biases - give me your hatred - give me your conditioned soul - and I will give you a unified and humane humanity. And by I, I mean You, for you are an image of me, just like I am an image of you - we are all reflections of each other in the vast mirror of motion and space.

As long as we move, we are able to reflect, but the moment you stop moving, you stop your soul from reflecting, thereafter you fall deep into the abyss of darkness, fear and doom. You are the life and you are the death - it is only motion that separates the two. Motion adds flavor to life, motion adds color to life, motion adds texture to life and motion places life in life.

You live so long as you move and if that motion is forward then you the soul turn more human and less animal, whereas if the motion is backward, then you turn more animal and less human. Choice is yours - whether you want to move ahead, that is, move in the process of recognizing and eliminating the shortcomings of today, or to move backward, that is, move in the process of justifying those shortcomings never to recognize their devastating impact upon the self and the society.

The reason that the society you live in is walking blind on the path of barbarism and stereotypical prejudices is because it is too primitively adamant to recognize its shortcomings and the shortcomings of its beloved ancestors. And they justify it in the name of cultural tradition and heritage. Tradition has become of more significance than peace and progress.

Every pattern or system of the society has its own traditions, and when the "stone-age" humans deny to accept even the possibility that some of those traditions might be keeping a people from moving ahead, a whole people become slaves to the chains of the pattern known as cultural heritage. So, break free my friend, and never let anyone put you in chains, be it in the name of culture, religion, politics, intellectualism or any other.

Patterns are not completely useless however - they have their own purpose and place in human life, which is to take away some of the thorns of risks from the path that a human walks on in everyday existence. As such the purpose of the pattern is to serve the humans, but today's so-called modern society takes the pattern to be of more value than the human, henceforth it makes slaves out of the humans to serve the pattern - and that's where all the troubles of the society begin - then to eliminate those troubles the humans create more patterns - thus the humans get ever-lastingly swallowed by the authoritarianism of patterns. Freedom can never arise from patterns that by their very nature take away freedom.

Patterns thrive on the insecurities of the humans, and the more a person turns loyal to a pattern, the more insecure the person becomes. In short insecurity brings loyalty and loyalty brings more insecurity, and as a result, the business of patterns keeps booming. However, here you must also remember that, not all people involved in this business are bad people - they simply are misled by their own delusions and insecurities. For example, not all politicians are bad human beings, not all psychics are bad human beings, not all faith-healers are bad human beings - these peddlers of psychological patterns, despite walking on the path of self-imposed delusions, might actually have the wellbeing of others in mind, nevertheless, the methods they chose only destroy the wellbeing of humanity and do nothing good in the long run.

The harsh reality of modern world is that almost every single puny human has become slave to a neurotic society filled with patterns. And no government, democratic or otherwise, no religion, progressive or ancient, and no ideology can bring progress in such a mentally degraded society. The only way forward is inward. Look inside - look inside, for the society has conditioned every single one of its members to look outside, and that is the reason behind all the conflicts, chaos and inequalities in the world.

Look inside my friend and break free from the charming influence of all the peddlers of patterns – don't discriminate against them, simply treat them with a genuine smile without engaging in a debate. Discuss if you want and have the patience and time, but don't debate.

I am not here to peddle you anything – I am not here to convert you either – I am here on earth to be an example of liberation – and if that example appeals to your civilized and conscientious psyche, then embrace it without judging other people's methods or the paths they walk on. If I have something good that appeals to your heart, then take it and put it to practice, for without practice all truths are worthless – without practice all heroism are inconsequential. Be a hero my friend, for your world needs you.

I am not a hero, and definitely not a messiah or a political leader and no, I am not a prophet - you know what I am - I am an idiot who thinks that all humans should think of themselves as humans above their tribal labels - I am just a fool, passing through time and space, being an embodiment of help, harmony and humanity. I don't need a religious institution, or a political party or an army to change the world, because I've got you, you the conscientious and caring individual, who can, despite all instinctual urges, look and step beyond humankind's innate tribalism.

You - your thoughts, your emotions, your actions are the real practical tools of peace and progress and not all the manifestos, doctrines, institutions and parties in the world. Remember, where there is politics, there can never be peace, and where there is peace, there's no need for politics. So, make your choice my friend, right this very moment - what exactly do you want - do you want just another excuse to keep the age-old nonsense of political conflicts going, or do you actually, genuinely, at the very core of your being, care about the manifestation of not a conceptual but an empirical peace in the human society! Make your choice, for peace and politics can never go hand in hand. You must let go of one to have the other.

So, let go, not just the pattern of politics but all patterns that keep you from growing – let go of all your grudges against the self and others. Mark you, the only way anyone can live in peace, is if they are willing to forgive both the self and others. If you just become some new cruel people, because you have been treated with cruelty by some old cruel people, and start treating others with cruelty, then they will end up becoming the new cruel people who will lead to many more generations of cruelty and violence. So, the cycle must break with you. Break the cycle my friend - break the cycle of violence, break the cycle of racism, break the cycle of bigotry. That's the only way all humans can live in peace.

I am a scientist, which means, I don't have the luxury to talk nonsense, if it can't pass the test of reasoning, no matter how much it sounds philosophical or spiritual. And simple reasoning makes it clear, that sometimes war may become the only resort available, but never try to justify it, by saying that it's the right thing to do, because war is never the right thing to do, no matter how right you feel. When you fire that first shot, you have no idea how many lives are going to be destroyed, no matter how right you feel. Once you fire that first shot you have no idea how many children will be orphaned. Once you fire that first shot you have no idea how many homes will be burnt to ashes.

So why not make an effort to break that savage habit of retaliation, and sit down together in order to understand each other beyond the petty little differences born of instinctual tribalism!

So, imagine me on my knees in front of you – bowing before your feet – and I say - I beg you, break the cycle now. Don't be obsessed with yet another revolution to overthrow the opposition, if you think that a violently excruciating revolution will make everything right. Let me ask a question about this brave new revolution of yours, when you have finally defeated all the bad guys and you've finally got it exactly the way you want it, what are you going to do with the individuals like you - the trouble-makers? How are you going to defend what you've achieved, against the next revolution? You may most blindly and boastfully proclaim that you will win. But remember, no one wins forever.

If you really, truly, genuinely care about the people around you, then throw away all that vengeance and hatred, and say to yourself - "no one shall have to feel what I have felt - no one shall have to bear the pain that I have borne - not on my watch". Break the cycle my friend - break the cycle by breaking the urge for yet another revolution, because the wheels only keep turning so long as you keep walking on the path of vengeance. Destroy that very vengeance at the very root of it and start a noble and novel life - a life of acceptance - a life of compassion - a life of conscience. And then you shall see, you've got a friend in everyone - and you'll be understood by everyone - listened to by everyone, just like you understand and listen to them. So, walk my friend, from now onward, the walk of peace, the walk of real liberty.

Mark you, light is not light that seeks light - goodness is not goodness that seeks advantage - virtue is not virtue that seeks reward. Light is light in the darkest hour - good is good in the deepest pit - virtue is only virtue in the extremes of hopelessness and misery. It is in the darkness that light is revealed. So, light your soul and lift the darkness around you. Burn yourself so that the cold world can have some warmth.

Be like water my friend - the water doesn't discriminate between a glass made of gold and a glass made of plastic - it just acquires the shape of whichever glass you pour it in - likewise be one with all humans regardless of their religion, race or social status, for in oneness lies bliss, in oneness lies progress. And if you ask why you should act in such a way, let me you tell you this - united you matter in the path of progress, divided you are no more civilized and progressive than the dogs on the street. United you gain the capacity to earn Mother Nature's respect for your existence, divided you gain cupcakes temporarily and an inevitable doom in the long run.

Now the real question is - do you want to live as a wise species - or do you want to be doomed like the dumb ferocious dinosaurs! The dinosaurs were perhaps the fiercest creatures that ever lived on earth, yet their fierceness couldn't ensure their survival. Force and fierceness are never the way. It is wisdom that paves the right way to life - to existence. Wisdom unites, whereas force divides. Love breathes life, whereas fierceness destroys life.

However, the truth of the situation is that force is the primary tool in the hands of the so-called politicians today, and they use it mostly not for the good of the people, but to chase after illusory ideologies while tearing this whole world apart into fragments. Politicians of today are fragmented beings creating a fragmented world. The fools of today's politics keep dividing the lands into more and more pieces, thinking that it would bring their people security, whereas the reality is, such an act only brings insecurity, as it leads to nothing but an increasing amount of conflicts.

Division can't bring peace and security, only assimilation can. Being civilized and sentient human has certain existential responsibilities, without which we might as well call ourselves dogs that urinate at the corner of the street and call it their territory. The world needs love, not borders. The resources invested in protecting the borders if put to use to uplift humanity then we could give all humans of the world all the happiness they require.

No peace can be lasting unless the humans become wise enough to need no borders, which can happen only if you all stop feeling threatened by your own kind and start fostering a sense of genuine trust for each other. I would rather be killed by you, the human, my own kind, than be killed by a disease. There is bliss in being killed by your own people. Once you recognize this simple revelation in your heart, then only can there be peace in the world. This doesn't mean that you are giving permission to your fellow human to kill you for no reason, rather you are showing in practice the absurd extent of your trust upon that person. Then it becomes extremely hard for the other person to see you as an enemy. That's the time when true oneness of all humans manifests within and among the humans, overwhelming all sectarian nonsense.

And remember, trust rarely begins from both sides simultaneously - one side must take the first step for the other to follow. You must show trust to see trust. The whole process of trust involves radiation and reflection. When you radiate trust, the other person will reflect that trust back to you, given that the person is in possession of healthy brain functioning.

Now the point is, there is no way for you to tell whether the other person does indeed possess healthy brain functioning, so let me tell you this - most humans do have enough healthy brain functioning available at the disposal of the self to reflect trust - so be not worried and take that leap of faith, for that is the kind of leap that's worth taking.

However, there is one kind of people from whom there is very little chance for your trust to be reflected, for they are too blinded by their bigotry - they are the fundamentalists. Now, whether you show trust to them or not, that's your decision. But I must warn you, you must be cautious of the people who deem books to be worth more than human life. You may choose to burn my books, and I won't mind a bit, but if you burn one of those books that the fundamentalists hold dear, then it's very likely that they won't even hesitate to kill you in the name of divine righteousness. And when those fundamentalists turn into political authorities, that's the worst thing that can happen to a young species such as ourselves.

The fundamentalists take pride in the exclusive supremacy of their own scriptures, the nationalists take pride in the exclusive greatness of their own national heritage, the so-called intellectuals take pride in the exclusive glory of their own field of work. And pride in one thing inadvertently brings along either subconscious or conscious condescension towards all other things belonging to other people.

Remember, by calling yourself American, European, Russian, Asian or anything else, you destroy the very fabric of humanity. Such an act might have proven essential for survival during our tribal days in the jungle, in the desert, in the caves, but now that we have finally become a global and apparently civilized species, it is time to get rid of such uncivilized, tribalistic primitiveness. So, stop being tribal and start being human. Then only you will be qualified to bring along with you your people on the path of humanity. And that walk of humanity is not going to be at all free from obstacles - it will be infested with countless thorns all along, and your soul will be replete with agonizing scars, by the time you either succeed in your mission or meet your doom, but be not defeated by the scars o brave soldier. The scars on your soul are the mark of your love for your people.

Keep your eyes both at the past, present and the future. Learn from the past, act in the present and construct the future. Remember, the fool only sees the present, but the wise sees all time collapsing and manifesting. Most politicians till now have solved not a single issue on this planet, because they have all been thinking as tribal leaders, instead of thinking as a responsible citizen of the world. So, act like a leader of your people with humility in your heart, but think as the whole of the humanity. Think and behave like the life of humanity depends on it, not just the lives of a few people in a small corner of the world.

Think about this – you are just cosmic dust moving through the vast ocean of space - and with that insignificance of existence, you dare waste your life on puny quarrels of religion, race and nationality. That's no way to live my friend - it may suit the creature of the jungle, but it doesn't suit the creature of the society. So, be one with your kind my friend, for in that oneness lies true civilization.

Be one and be civilized. By civilized I don't mean that phony kind of civilized pretense where you pretend to be egalitarian, yet the moment your kid brings home a partner of color, or of a different religion, you instantaneously burst out in shock and try either to break them apart by all cheap means available, or to convert your future in-law into your own religion. Such primitive act is no different from the acts of terrorism. Civilized behavior must be felt in your bones and practiced every moment of your life in the progress of both the individual as well as the society. You are the society, the society is you.

So, stop quarreling, once and for all, because once you stop quarreling, your children will stop quarreling, and then their children - and slowly the world will eventually turn into a real civilized, sentient and serene society. Your ancestors tore this whole world apart into pieces and now you are doing the same. Don't repeat their mistakes my friend and take control of your world - not your neighborhood, or your state or your country - but your world, because the whole world is your family. My Christianity is the best and your Islam is the worst - my America is the best and your Russia is the worst - my India is the best and your Pakistan is the worst - my Bulgaria is the best and your Turkey is the worst - my Britain is the best and your France is the worst - stop this 'mine and yours' business once and for all and start thinking as 'ours' - our America - our Russia - our Christianity - our Islam - our Britain - our France - our Bulgaria - our Turkey - all of it either belongs to all of us or to none of us. Stop thinking tribal and start thinking human.

Peace doesn't come by fighting - it comes by not fighting - it comes by not hitting back in return. However, the instinctual urge for hitting back in return cannot be erased from our neurobiology right away, as we are still highly driven by our amygdaloid responses, but if enough generations conscientiously refrain from hitting back in return, for enough millennia, then in time, that very harmful instinct would vanish from human nature. Now the question is, how would all this psychological trickery can be made possible! The answer is, it all begins with you - one being conscientious enough to not hit back in return.

One human's despair is all humans' despair - one human's joy is all humans' joy - one human's accomplishments is all humans' accomplishments. Such should be the genuine thinking of a civilized and conscientious human, if there is to be peace and harmony in the world. Harmony can never manifest unless the humans are willing to let go of some of their personal fulfilments impeding acceptance, for the betterment of the species.

There was a time when members of a tribe were required to see benefits of their tribe of more significance than personal fulfilments, which ensured a bitter-sweet survival of that specific tribe over the survival of other tribes. But now that our tribal days are over, we stand at yet another crossroads in the history of human evolution - now we must make a choice, not as tribalistic ape-men but as conscientious human - we must make a choice whether our own country, our own religion, our own language, our own skin color, our own cultural heritage is more important to us than anything else, or are we going to finally let go of our instinctual tribalistic traits and be humans above all sectarian identities.

Now here is the magnastic choicelessness of the matter. If we give in to tribal loyalty like our primitive ancestors did, then we shall make a world no more civilized and peaceful than the wild and vicious environment that our ancestors lived in, however, if - just if, we could with all our conscience give up such loyalty and see all humans as our own family, then my friend, our world - the human world, can become something majestic - something surreal yet completely real – something which we today only dream of and wish for, but will be a reality for our future generations - our children, grandchildren and their children. Now comes the most crucial question of all - are you ready - are you ready to give up your identity - your identity as American, Russian, African, Christian, Jew, Muslim, Atheist, or white, black, brown or anything else! In your very answer - and in your action upon that answer - lies the seed for peace on earth.

And this action is no big thing if you can truly see with the eyes of your entire cognitive realm the devastation that the tribal identities bring along in the world around us - once you see this - really see this - then the significance of those identities and their correlated psychological loyalty would automatically begin to fade away from your psyche, as the brain circuits related to all this change forever. Allow me to give you an example to show you how this happens at the neurological level. Let's change some of your brain circuits right this very moment, shall we! Gaze at this picture for a few seconds.

Figure 2.1 Random jumble of splotches
(Tovee, Rolls and Ramachandran, 1996)

Eventually, but not right away, you will see a Dalmatian dog sniffing the ground mottled with shadows of leaves. Once the dog has been seen, it is impossible to get rid of that perception of the dog from the picture. Neurons in the temporal lobes of your brain become altered permanently after the initial brief exposure, once you have "seen" the dog. Our perception of so-called reality is constantly changing, for our very mind, is constantly changing - constantly evolving. Every moment, we create a new reality, and then the earlier reality loses its accountability.

So, if you can actually see a world full of harmony, beyond the tribal world filled with tribal hatred and conflicts, it would automatically become your reality, and that reality of your mind would outpour into the world through your actions, thus it would become the reality of the world you live in. It all begins with perception and realization.

Remember, your perception is the world's perception, your realization is the world's realization. So, never ever say again that the world is too big to change - and that you must follow the rules of the world, in order to be a part of it - start being the change yourself, and the world will change - see the rules that harm the society and overwhelm them with reasoning, compassion and conscience, and they will cease to exist, perhaps slowly, but inevitably. And be aware not to make new rules after breaking the old harmful ones - observe all things around you and be aware of them - that's all you need to sustain peace and harmony in the world, and in such a world rules would no longer be a necessity - in such a world law will become a matter of primitive history.

What you call law is essentially the need of an uncivilized and unfree society. A truly civilized and free society needs no law. The presence of law is not the sign of order, but it is the sign of disorder. Hence, the true purpose of law should not be to maintain order, rather it should be to create a truly lawless society. Order lies in lawlessness, whereas in law lies disorder. So, does this mean, we should get rid of law all together! Before we attempt to investigate the answer to this question, we must first understand what law really is and what kind of impact it has upon the internal realm of the human society.

Law is an illusory perceptual structure, a pattern, built by humans to depict the acceptable and non-acceptable behavior of humans in a certain society. This structure defines for all humans in a specific society, what is right and what is wrong. Now the question is, on what grounds does law define the righteousness of its own depictions! Lawmakers, who rarely have an insight of a truly progressive and civilized society, decide on the perimeters of law based on their biases and knacks, and rarely on actual scientific evidence. It's like asking the blind to show the path. So, for law to be of actual use in the society at our current evolutionary stage, it must be cooked in the vessel of scientific findings with the fire of reasoning and compassion.

Science is the most effective tool we have as a species in the path of progress, so regardless of your scientific or non-scientific background, always try your best to stay updated with scientific findings, for these findings aid us in our understanding of various phenomena of the world, which helps us in the process of being a being of awareness and conscience.

Let me elaborate on this matter a little further. Imagine, you are a genuine human with a functional civilized conscience and very little familiarity with scientific findings, and you see no problems in the parenting of a gay couple, and now imagine another human-looking ape full with stereotypical prejudices and bigotry and very little awareness of scientific findings, who most proudly proclaims gay couples to be unfit parents. Here no matter which one is the right one, both of you are unfamiliar with scientific findings on the actual matter of parental capacity of homosexual couples, so neither of you can actually prove your statement, it's merely all a matter of unfounded opinions.

But if you could actually have a basic scientific understanding of the whole matter of homosexuality, then you could not only feel that the homosexual parents are just as competent as heterosexual couple, but you could actually see it as an empirical truth of the natural kingdom beyond all doubts and confusions. Basic scientific understanding of a phenomenon enhances your perception of that phenomenon and widens your vision of the world within and the world without.

Now since we talked a little bit about understanding the phenomenon of homosexual parenting, allow me to bring up an excerpt on this matter from my treatise on homosexuality "Either Civilized or Phobic".

> *The most intriguing feature of Homosexual behavior is that it is in no way different than heterosexual behavior in terms of psychological dynamics as well as parental ability. Let's take humans for example. The psychological dynamics of heterosexual and homosexual relationships are just the same regardless of what you hear from the stupid and superstitious part of the population. Which means, there is no difference in the true sensation of love between a heterosexual couple and a homosexual couple. The psychological adjustments made by the partners are just the same in both heterosexual and homosexual relationships. Even in terms of duration of the relationship, same-sex partners stay together*

for 20 years or even longer, just like heterosexual partners.

And as for parental capabilities, despite the baseless claims of those who oppose gay parents, no empirical study shows that having a gay male or lesbian parent is deleterious to children. Consequently, a growing number of courts have finally started to regard sexual orientation as irrelevant to a parent's ability to provide a good and healthy upbringing for his or her children.

In the 1990s, an unprecedented number of homosexual women and men chose to become parents in committed homosexual relationships. Many homosexual men and women had been parents before this time, but their children were usually conceived in a heterosexual marriage. Homosexual parents have often faced hostility from the conservative and apparently blind parts of the society, and have even been denied custody of their own children in many cases. If this is what we call civilization, then I am afraid we are no more civilized than the bonobos. Discriminations are never a sign of a civilized society. What makes us civilized is our act of liberated kindness with other people beyond the man-made primitive citadels of gender, race, religion and sexual orientation.

Sexual orientation defines only sexual orientation, nothing else. It does not define a person's mental capacities. It does not define a person's passions. And above all, it does not define a person's character.

In 1956, Chicago, a young psychologist named Evelyn Hooker (yes, that was her name) presented a study to a meeting of the American Psychological Association. She herself during her training routinely studied the so-called theory of homosexuality as a pathology. A group of young gay men with whom she had become friendly seemed, however, to be quite healthy and lucid in all daily activities. It suddenly appeared to Hooker that the scientific community still didn't know about Homosexuality. So, she received a study grant from the National Institute of Mental Health and chose a group of thirty gay men as the objects of her research and thirty straight men as controls. None of the sixty had ever sought or undergone psychiatric treatment. It was the first time that homosexuals had been studied outside a medical setting or prison.

She conducted psychological tests on her sixty subjects, including the Rorschach ink-blot test, producing sixty psychological profiles. She removed all identifying marks, including those indicating sexual orientation. In order to eliminate her own biases, she gave them for interpretation to three eminent psychologists. One of them was Bruno Klopfer, who believed that he would be able to distinguish homosexuals from heterosexuals by means of the Rorschach test. However, quite astonishingly, none of the three could differentiate the homosexuals from the heterosexuals. In side-by-side comparisons of matched profiles, the heterosexuals and homosexuals were indistinguishable, demonstrating an equal distribution of pathology and mental health.

Hence, Hooker concluded from the study that homosexuality did not constitute a clinical entity and that it was not associated with pathology whatsoever. Her research was driven by her strong then-unconventional belief that for psychiatry to be minimally scientific, pathology must be defined in a way that is objective and empirically observable. Her findings were subsequently replicated in numerous empirical studies of both women and men. The weight of growing empirical evidence, coupled with changing social norms and the development of politically active gay community in the United States of America, compelled the Directors of the American Psychiatric Association to officially remove homosexuality from the Diagnostic and Statistical Manual, in 1973.

The movement to declassify homosexuality as a diagnosis has been strongly supported by the American Psychological Association (APA.) ever since 1974. APA has passed numerous legal resolutions to support equal right for lesbians and gay men in employment, child custody and access to services.

However, there is still a huge difference between theory and practice. Humans shall always remain humans, no matter the position of science. Ever since 1973, the scientific approach among the mainstream psychotherapists has been to help the homosexual clients adjust successfully to their sexual orientation and live life to the fullest. Despite all this, some (non-)psychotherapists and religious counselors continue to make disgraceful attempts to convert homosexuals into heterosexuals.

Regardless of all this, after conducting relentless neurobiological studies, on the biological foundation of sexual orientation, we have been able to move Homosexuality from the domain of psychiatric illnesses into the realm of normal variants of human sexual behavior. And the resulting fact of such an accomplishment is this:

Homosexuality is immutable, irreversible and nonpathological.

A particular sexual orientation is no way an indication of either good or evil. It is not the gender of the two individuals in a relationship that matters, but the content of that relationship. Is there violence in the relationship? Is there enslavement of one partner by the other? Is the relationship a healthy place for the growth of both partners involved? These should be the standards with which relationships all sexual orientations should be measured.

- ***Either Civilized or Phobic: A Treatise on Homosexuality, 2017***

So, the next time you encounter a homophobic, say to them with utmost awareness of the phenomenon of homosexuality, being homosexual is no more abnormal than being lefthanded. Be the lamp of egalitarianism my friend, in a society filled with various disgusting forms of barbarian prejudices. And remember, science in its truest form is and will always remain compatible with human rights and equality. So, strengthen your tools of reasoning in the purifying fire of scientific findings and put them to use in the demolition of prejudices and discriminations, be it racial, sexual, religious, political, intellectual or any other. And this is not at all going to be an easy job, in fact, your path will be filled with the thorns of misery and mockery – yet you must go on, for the fate of humanity is at stake here.

When the candle burns bright, all you can see is the light it radiates, but what you can't see is the soul-crunching agony of that candle - agony you can't even dare to imagine. Agony can bring greatness out of a person, but in the process, the person has to walk barefoot on red-hot coal while bleeding from all over the being. And thus the agony of the braveheart delivers humanity the gift of peace and progress.

Peacemaking is not like lovemaking, that you feel turned on to carry out for a few minutes, or alas seconds, and then feel chirpy, in case of a woman, or sleepy, in case of a man - peacemaking is the endeavor of a lifetime. Every day of your life, every minute of your day, every second of those minutes, you have to think peace, speak peace and act peace. Only then, will there be hope for peace. Shouting about world peace in the general assembly won't bring peace in the world, unless each one of us humans, recognizes and realizes the true beauty of unification and acceptance.

Acceptance will bring peace by itself, whether you talk about peace or not. So, shift your focus from the issue called "peace" for the time being, and place it upon the simple everyday action of acceptance. Build your whole being on the edifice of acceptance, and there will no longer be any need for pompous organizations to bring peace on earth. Organizations can't bring peace, for peace begins with the individual - it begins with you. And so long as you rely on these organizations to bring peace in your surroundings, peace shall remain merely an issue for the celebrities to exploit as a means to attract more followers.

It pains me to say, that almost all of humanity has become obsessed with the pompous and fake glory of fame, that's why the dumbest words of the famous appear wise and the wisest words of the commoner seem dumb. Such is the society you live in - such is the society we all are proud to be a part of - shame on us! Charisma is not the measure of greatness, character is, and this character of the everyday individual must get to work with all the powers in the veins to actually radiate peace, kindness and harmony all around. It doesn't matter whether you are a janitor, a teacher, a scientist, a sex worker, or anything else - what matters is that you are a human - and that's precisely what the world needs in order to be truly, genuinely peaceful.

Being in peace doesn't mean absence of misery, it means absence of conflict in the mind. There are two kinds of misery in the world, first and the rare one is that which comes along in the path of greatness and change, and the other one which has actually become an infection in today's so-called modern society, the one that is self-imposed - the one that is caused by the self, due to lack of insight both within and without. The first kind of misery is healthy and quite necessary if one is to truly, genuinely make a civilized and conscientious world, whereas the other one is illusory and rather ridiculous, for it only exists so long as the mind stays ignorant of its own capacities.

I see what the humans could achieve if only they knew themselves, and by knowing themselves, I am not referring to a kind of mystical nonsensical illusory knowledge, rather I am simply referring to the plain, ordinary everyday awareness of oneself. And since I see what humanity could achieve, I couldn't sit still - I chose at my own free will to pay no heed to the needs of my body, so that my kind, my own species could have a better world to live in. Hence, I am in misery, I am in pain, but I am not in conflict.

Naskar the person died long ago, now what lives in front of you, and indeed within you, is Naskar the idea - the idea of one humanity - the idea of a harmonious humanity - a humanity that places the benefit of the neighbor above the benefit of the self - a humanity that places the significance of shared joy above the joy of the individual - a humanity that lives not in a chaotic planet, but in a truly intertwined conscientious society. A civilized society should mean non-judgmental communication - it should mean warm interconnection - it should mean shared psychology - it should mean a true psychological singularity. The world needs psychological singularity, that is oneness among humans, not some pompous biotechnological singularity.

And this singularity - this utterly natural psychological singularity or oneness can only manifest if you the individual - the indivisible force of being is free from all sorts of internal divisions and segregations. With the sense of internal oneness rises the true change – the true progress in the external world - henceforth, everything would be alright for the human species. Everyone says they wish that everything could be alright for everyone. The fact is, everything would be alright for everyone, if only people could learn to behave like human beings.

Now you may wonder what does behaving like a human being mean! That is the real question here isn't it! The answer however, must - I repeat - the answer must rise from your own mind, because only then it would have real, practical impact upon your life and the lives you touch with your presence.

The answer could be discovered in the very question. Behaving like a human being means behaving as a human being and not as lesser creatures that only look human. Behaving as a human being means acting as a human being and nothing short of that. Rest you must figure out yourself using all the powers of your psyche, for I am not here to preach or teach you anything.

I am no religious preacher, or a spiritual teacher, nor am I an intellectual philosopher or a divine incarnation - I am you in the service of you. Serve my would-be patriot - serve your people - your kind – serve your humans like your life depends on it - serve with all the might in your body and brain - serve with your whole being - make your existence a cynosure of service - and then only shall evolution pave the path toward a less wild and more humane world.

Service of humanity is practical divinity - there is nothing else - it is all about your action for the benefit of your kind - it's that simple - this very simplicity is what adds glory to your divinity - this very simplicity adds glory to the fabric of humanity. The existence of the fabric of humanity is predicated on the liberated actions of the liberated humans. And liberated are those who are fully conscious of the indomitable spirit that lies within them - the sacred power of greatness and glory. There is no greater sacred power than the indomitable spirit of humanity. And you my friend, are that humanity.

And here please don't get drowned in the primitive thoughts about mind, body and spirit. Mystics would tell you, you are not your body - materialists would tell you, you are only your body - whereas the existential fact of human life is that, you are not your body - you are not your mind - you are nothing - for there is nothing constant about you at any given moment that you can say that you are that - your mind is constantly changing - your body is constantly changing - you as a bio-psychological creature are constantly evolving - if there is anything that's constant about you, it's change itself -

therefore, what you really are, is an eternal force of change. And with that force of change, o my brave soldier of progress, you can bring a tsunami of kindness and reasoning in the farthest corners of the world.

You are the change, once you realize that, the world is bound to change. So, destroy yourself if needed to be the change that every meek human only prays for. With destruction of your very identity, will the world see, not a new dawn, for there never was a real dawn, but the true dawn - the dawn of compassion - the dawn of conscience - the dawn of egalitarianism and an empirical harmony.

Egalitarianism is not an ideology or a philosophical concept - it is simply a pompous word referring to the non-pompous truth of human uniformity. It is the truth that humanity has taken for granted, and as a result, they are constantly fighting among themselves in the name of tribalistic ideologies. It pains me to say this, today's humans only look human, but act like animals. They judge before they understand - they conclude before they realize - they proclaim before they recognize. They talk about harmony yet in their psyche they are more broken and conflicted than a broken glass. As a result, harmony has become yet another pompous ideology for them to take pride in, without sacrificing anything on their part - they simply talk about harmony while desperately clinging to their own beloved tribal labels and expect peace to manifest magically out of thin air. That's not how harmony works my friend.

Global harmony is only the reflection of humankind's internal harmony. Until the humans turn whole human beings tearing apart all their tribal labels, harmony can never be an empirical reality of the planet we live in. So, now the time has come, to slowly let go of your loyalty to the label that your environment has imposed on you. Let go of your label, for a beautiful, peaceful, harmonious world is waiting right around the corner. Remember my friend, peace first, sophistication later. Harmony first, luxury later. Peace is more a matter of deep psychological realization than of arduous physical effort.

Peace is not something you can make, rather it is something which you simply become. Be the peace incarnate and you'll see peace in the world. Every footstep that you take, every word that you utter, every act that you commit, must shine with the radiant and priceless jewels of peace, only then there shall be peace on earth. And for this, if you need to sacrifice yourself and all your bodily desires, then do so with utmost glory, for what could be more glorious than to give your life for your kind. Burn yourself so that the cold world can have some warmth. I did so - countless more did before me - and infinitely more will need to do so after me - so, why can't it be you. I gave up living as a person, so that you can have a humane and conscientious world to live in - and in return I ask nothing from you, except that you live as a whole human being.

Remember my friend, everybody wants to have a family of their own, but what about the greater family called humanity beyond the personal domain of individual existence! Who will take care of them, if not you! Your blood is full with vigor my brave soldier of destiny, so bring all that vigor out in the service of your family called humanity. Be the new dreamer of a unified dream - the new visionary of a humanitarian vision - the new braveheart with courage unseen.

Every generation needs caretakers - and the caretaker of your generation is you. Be the caretaker of humanity - a real living embodiment of godly prowess and potential. Be the observer of all, but never the follower to anyone, for loyalty brings destruction both in the self and the society. To live with the head held high, one must leave loyalty. In freedom, lies salvation - in freedom lies evolution - in freedom lies absolution - and above all, in freedom lies truth. Be free and think the truth - act the truth - live the truth.

Here, a conscientious human might come up with the genuinely curios question - what is this truth business whatsoever and why is it so damn important in the first place! That's precisely the point - truth is not a mere business issue, nor is it merely important to humans.

Truth is the indomitable force of evolution - the force that guides you in the journey of liberty and humaneness. Without truth, time is merely the kingdom of the animals. Time brings progress and humanitarian glory, only if truth walks the nerves of our mind, as we walk the alleys of space - in that walk we relinquish the space between the self and the other. The space between human and human is the most devastating delusion of all. I could call it an illusion, if it didn't do any harm to human existence, but it does the most disgraceful harm of all, that is, impeding in the harmonious progress of humanity.

Humanity without harmony is more dangerous to itself than the t-rex was to other creatures. So, this harmony cannot be perceived any longer as an intellectual endeavor of the intellectual portions of human population - it must go deep into the veins of every single sentient human and make them realize their uniformity - their unity - their absolute divinity.

Divine you are not, but divine you can be, the moment you realize the divinity bursting within you with its ever-glorious radiance of conscience and compassion. So, throw away all mystical nonsense and be divine through your acts of kindness - be divine through your gestures of acceptance - be divine through your footsteps of awareness. One life is all you've got - so put that life to some real impactful use - put it to use, not abuse, for all acts of non-use are abuse, when we are talking about the force of life.

Human life is precious, for it has the potential to achieve things that no other creature can, for they lack the brain capacity to do so. Human life is the only force of life on this planet biologically capable of becoming the caretaker of all creatures on earth, not just its own kind. So, be kind and take all the burden of your kind on your own shoulders. Accept others with all their pros and cons and take them with you in the path of right living.

Someone asked me the other day - 'could you tell me, what is right human living' - I put my hand on his shoulder and asked him to sit beside me, with a gentle smile on my face, then uttered softly, 'I don't know your religious belief or disbelief, I don't know your professional background, I don't know your economic or social status, all I need to know is that you are a human being, a reflection of my own self, so I treat you with kindness and acceptance, same as I treat myself'. The world is flooded with judgments and opinions - for once my friend, take a step beyond that flood, and you shall see a beautiful world, where being human is a beautiful thing - in that world being human is all that matters.

So, forget the tribal labels and tribal loyalties and simply be a human. So long as you remain tribal, world peace will not be a truth of the human world. So, make your choice - what's more important to you - your primitive tribalism or world peace. World peace can only be forged out of the nerves of liberated humans. In short, it's only the humans who can create a peaceful world, not tribal apes.

Now the question is, what kind of a being can be hailed as a human. A human is the one, who sees the self in others. All humans are images of your own self - their pain is your pain - their misery is your misery - their sorrows are your sorrows - so rise and be the hope, help and joy in their lives! Do you realize it - not theoretically, but actually, at the very core of your spine - do you! If you do, my friend, then and then only, you are a human, in every other case you are just another animal on a planet called earth. Human existence is not a luxury to be wasted in the futile pursuit of artificial possessions - human existence is the most glorious privilege, and as such it must be valued and put to practice in the most productive and progressive manner.

And the first step of this progressive and productive practice of human life force is the recognition and expulsion of nonsensical thinking. Now here is the interesting part - you can't really get rid of any thought from your mind by force, you can only overwhelm it with another more psychologically powerful thought, and when you let that thought be born of reasoning and humanitarian cognitive processes, then the predominant nonsensical thoughts of your mind automatically lose their grip over your psyche, and slowly their underlying neuronal circuits fade away and with them those thoughts.

So, darkness cannot be expelled with force, it can only be overwhelmed with light - ignorance and delusions cannot be expelled with force, they can only be overwhelmed with knowledge. And this process of overwhelming ignorance and delusions with knowledge is the practical enlightenment of a thinking society. And this is a ceaseless process - which means enlightenment doesn't just happen for a few seconds, it is a never-ending process of psychological growth. Now let's deeper into this matter.

What is enlightenment? Please, don't already assume that you know the answer. Enlightenment is a very complicated term in the human society and rather a venerated one, despite the fact that most humans never in their lifetime actually consciously understand or experience that enlightenment. The human society does not experience enlightenment, yet they assume that it is something extraordinary and rather glorious to talk about in intellectual groups. In today's society, the idea of enlightenment is merely an idea, to be talked and debated about over a cup of coffee. And that's precisely what makes the humans incapable of actually experiencing a real revelatory enlightenment.

So, let's ask the real question - what is enlightenment? And the answer can be discovered in two folds. There is not one, but two versions of enlightenment - one is the transcendental state of oneness, which I termed in my book What is Mind, as "Absolute Unitary Qualia", and the other one is a plain ordinary non-mystical sense of oneness among the humans, the singularity we talked about earlier.

The transcendental form of enlightenment is what led most of the religious giants to eventually walk on the path of humanitarian glory and be at the service of the humans. However, this transcendental experience does not occur in ordinary circumstances, for it requires specific internal or/and external stimuli, hence in the modern sentient world it is more practical and progressive to focus on its practical implication instead, which is an everyday sense of uniformity and unity among all humans.

So, in simple terms, time has changed, so should the human perception of enlightenment. All that really matters is that you do not raise any sort of wall between you and the other humans - and that should be the real practical enlightenment of the civilized and conscientious society. You don't need to renounce your everyday life and become a wandering monk in order to have enlightenment. If you have realized your responsibility towards your society, then you are more enlightened that all the priests, imams and pundits combined.

I once renounced my home in Calcutta, and roamed around the villages of Bengal as a monk. But after I attained the Absolute Divine state of Unification with the Universe, I realized that the purpose of life is not renunciation of anything, but the realization of the purpose itself. Ask yourself, what is the purpose of your life, not in terms of destiny or fate, but in terms of fulfillment of your life. Don't let the illusion of destiny keep you from doing what you love to do - for nothing is meant to be, or not to be - it is only your willful and persistent action that determines your destiny. Your life is your decision - your destiny is your decision. So, rise and start working.

Be the harmony in the melody echoing in the heart of humanity. And remember not to criticize anyone, even if that person's head is filled with mystical garbage, for criticism only acquires criticism in return - it is only with acceptance, that there is hope for receiving acceptance in return - acceptance is the first step towards the recovery of the soul from the illness of mysticism. Be enlightened, not with mystical nonsense, but with actual awareness of the self and the society. As I have said in my last book on medical philosophy,

> *real enlightenment is not at all free from all sorts of ignorance, but it is at all times aware of that ignorance as well as all the shortcomings of the self, whereas in the so-called enlightenment fueled by mysticism, the*

self gets consumed by the illusion of knowledge, which is worse than ignorance.

You can be a scientist and an enlightened being, you can be a teacher and an enlightened being, you can be a trucker and an enlightened being, you can be a janitor or an entertainer and an enlightened being, you can be a sex worker and an enlightened being. In fact, an enlightened being is a thousand times better at whatever he or she does, for an enlightened being is simply a being of awareness. And awareness brings insight - then that insight brings peace, progress and humanity both in the world within and the world without.

Awareness is the only glue that can keep the fabric of humanity intact - in fact, the fabric of humanity is torn apart into pieces due to the lack of this awareness. Be aware and true oneness among the humans shall rise quite naturally, without force, without planning, without effort. Once the humans implode with pride-less awareness, humanity will explode with egalitarian and progressive greatness.

With that explosion of egalitarianism and true conscientious progress, the fabric of humanity shall rise triumphant as one unified and uniform species, not once again, but for the first time in the history of life on earth. In this unification lies the true liberty for each human and all humans. The separation between human and human is born from the scarcity of this liberty. And as a result, the frog in the well knows nothing more grand than its own tiny well and perceives frogs from elsewhere as not its own kind, but mere "foreigners". But once you break that illusory wall of the well that your culture has built for you, then freedom will implode within you quite instantly. And that freedom by its very nature brings acceptance.

Remember, the highest creed is Universal Acceptance. There is nothing higher than this. Plenty are the tastes and plenty are the paths. But try not to pay attention to the path that another person is walking on, rather try to pay attention to that person's behavior with other people, for, whatever the path may be, that a person walks on, if he or she has kindness and acceptance for another person, then there is no greater being than that.

And the most important natural factor here to remember at your very core is that, Nature never lends a hand in the attainment of greatness - it only puts obstacles in your path - but only if you have the persistence to keep moving ahead through all those obstacles bearing unimaginable agony, will greatness kiss your feet. It's not a matter of if, it's only a matter of when.

Be destroyed my brave patriot of humanity to undo the destruction brought upon this world by our ancestors. Our ancestors were too busy fighting in the name of tribalism, to notice the bliss that comes from collective delight. So, once and for all, stop fighting and start delighting. We must delight together as a species or perish alone as insects. Be mad, my dear sibling - be mad to make that collective delight a reality - be mad to make collective good a reality. If everyone had the madness for doing good, there wouldn't be any misery in the world.

Only if the humans could realize the inexplicable happiness that comes from loving others, there would no longer be any trace of hatred and discrimination in the world. Love my friend - love beyond all conditions - be the ocean of love - be the sea of compassion - be the continent of conscience - and no puny ape will have the power to raise walls among the humans and weaken the fabric of humanity, for love strengthens the spirit of humanity beyond all innate weaknesses.

There is no greater sacred power than the indomitable spirit of humanity. And that spirit has no nationality - it has no race - it has no religion or any other sort of cheap uncivilized labels. Forget not my would-be patriot, label-less humanity is true humanity.

"Humanity" it's not just a word - it's a word with the highest responsibility - it carries the responsibility to be the torch of conscience - and the fuel for that torch comes from the deepest fathoms of your soul - the soul of the individual - so, the only way to keep it burning and indeed to make it burn brighter is to enhance the flow of conscience in your own veins with the elixir of awareness.

SONNET OF MIND

Sonnet of Mind

Goodness is godliness,

For in being good you become the God,

Sectarianism brings loneliness,

For joy rises when you stop being an intellectual fraud,

Peace and joy can't be bought,

For you buy something when you don't own it,

Jewels of bliss are with which your mind is already fraught,

All you need is to realize within and recognize it,

With realization comes contentment,

For contentment is the product of awareness,

So be aware with all your might transcendent,

And be the being of a conscientious consciousness,

Consciousness is possessed by all animals but without consequence,

It's only the human mind that holds the power to create an all-pervading influence.

SONNET OF SAPIENS

Sonnet of Sapiens

No religion is greater than love,

For love is the embodiment of divinity,

No church is higher than the self,

Cause the self is the manifestation of the Almighty,

No worship is greater than help,

For helping is the service of God,

No prayer is as sacred as kindness,

For in kindness lies the real act of the Lord,

No scripture is more glorious than the mind,

For the mind is the creator of the scriptures,

So learn from that scripture within to be of help to your kind,

And be the glue to the fabric of humanity healing all ruptures,

Heal your kind my friend with your wisdom and warmth transcendent,

If not you then who else will unify humanity and rise as sapiens triumphant.

BIBLIOGRAPHY

Aristotle. Politics. Penguin; Revised, Reprint edition. (2000)

Aristotle. De Anima (On the Soul). Penguin Random House. 1987

Aristotle. Physics. Kessinger Publishing, 2004

Adolphs R (2003) Cognitive neuroscience of human social behaviour. Nature Rev Neurosci 4: 165–178.

Adolphs R, Damasio H, Tranel D, Cooper G, Damasio AR (2000) A role for somatosensory cortices in the visual recognition of emotion as revealed by three-dimensional lesion mapping. J Neurosci 20: 2683–2690.

Adolphs R, Tranel D, Damasio AR (2003) Dissociable neural systems for recognizing emotions. Brain Cogn 52: 61–69.

Afton, A. D. (1985). Forced copulation as a reproductive strategy of male lesser scaup: A field test of some predictions. - Behaviour 92, p. 146-167.

Allison T, Puce A, McCarthy G. (2000) Social perception from visual cues: role of the STS region. Trends Cogn Sci 4: 267–278.

Andresen, Jensine, and Robert Forman, eds. Cognitive Models and Spiritual Maps. Bowling Green, Ohio: Imprint Academic, 2000.

Ashbrook, James, and Carol Albright. The Humanizing Brain: Where Religion and Neuroscience Meet. Cleveland, OH: Pilgrim Press, 1997.

Azari, Nina, Janpeter Nickel, Gilbert Wunderlich, Michael Niedeggen, Harald Hefter, Lutz Tellmann, Hans Herzog, Petra Stoerig, Dieter Birnbacher, and Rudiger Seitz. "Neural Correlates of Religious Experience."

European Journal of Neuroscience 13, no. 8 (2001)

Agar, N. (2004). Liberal eugenics: In defence of human enhancement. London: Blackwell Publishing.

Alteheld, N., Roessler, G., Vobig, M., & Walter, R. (2004). The retina implant new approach to a visual prosthesis. Biomedizinische Technik, 49(4), 99–103.

Antal, A., Nitsche, M. A., Kincses, T. Z., Kruse, W., Hoffmann, K. P., & Paulus, W. (2004a). Facilitation of visuo-motor learning by transcranial direct current stimulation of the motor and extrastriate visual areas in humans. European Journal of Neuroscience, 19(10), 2888–2892.

Augustine JR (1996) Circuitry and functional aspects of the insular lobe in primates including humans. Brain Res Rev 22: 229–244.

Barash, D. P. (1977). Sociobiology of rape in mallards (Anas platyrhynchos): Responses of the mated male. - Science 197, p. 788-789.

Barthalomew, G. A. (1970). A model for the evolution of pinniped polygyny. - Evolution 24, p. 546-559.

Berger, J. (1986). Wild horses of the great basin: Social competition and population size. - The University of Chicago Press, Chicago.

Birkhead, T. R., Johnson, S. D. & Nettleship, D. N. (1985). Extra-pair matings and mate guarding in the common murre Uria aalge. - Anim. Behav. 33, p. 608-619.

Beauregard, Mario, and Vincent Paquette. "Neural Correlates of a Mystical Experience in Carmelite Nuns." Neuroscience Letters 405, no. 3 (2006)

Benson, Herbert. Timeless Healing: The Power and Biology of Belief. New York: Scribner, 1996

Bogen, J.E.(1995a), 'On the neurophysiology of consciousness: Part I. An overview', Consciousness and Cognition, 4.

Bogen, J.E. (1995b), 'On the neurophysiology of consciousness: Part II. Constraining the semantic problem', Consciousness and Cognition, 4.

Bremner, J. D., R. Soufer, et al. (2001). "Gender differences in cognitive and neural correlates of remembrance of emotional words." Psychopharmacol Bull 35 (3).

Brothers, L. (2002). The social brain: A project for integrating primate behavior and neurophysiology in a new domain. In J. T. Cacioppo et al. (Eds.), Foundations in neuroscience. Cambridge, MA: MIT Press.

Buss, D. D. (2003). Evolutionary Psychology: The New Science of Mind, 2nd ed. New York: Allyn & Bacon.

Buss, D. M. (1989). "Conflict between the sexes: Strategic interference and the evocation of anger and upset." J Pers Soc Psychol 56 (5).

Buss, D. M. (1995). "Psychological sex differences. Origins through sexual selection." Am Psychol 50 (3).

Buss, D. M. (2002). "Review: Human Mate Guarding." Neuro Endocrinol Lett 23 (Suppl 4).

Buss, D. M., and D. P. Schmitt (1993). "Sexual strategies theory: An evolutionary perspective on human mating." Psychol Rev 100 (2).

Blakemore SJ, Decety J (2001) From the perception of action to the understanding of intention. Nature Rev Neurosci 2: 561.

Bruce C, Desimone R, Gross CG (1981) Visual properties of neurons in a polysensory area in superior temporal sulcus of the macaque. J Neurophysiol 46: 369–384.

Buccino G, Binkofski F, Fink GR, Fadiga L, Fogassi L, Gallese V, Seitz RJ, Zilles K, Rizzolatti G, Freund HJ (2001) Action observation activates premotor and parietal areas in a somatotopic manner: an fMRI study. Eur J Neurosci 13: 400–404.

Buccino G, Vogt S, Ritzl A, Fink GR, Zilles K, Freund HJ, Rizzolatti G (2004) Neural circuits underlying imitation of hand actions: an event related fMRI study. Neuron 42: 323–34.

Calder AJ, Keane J, Manes F, Antoun N, Young AW (2000) Impaired recognition and experience of disgust following brain injury. Nature Neurosci 3: 1077–1078.

Carey DP, Perrett DI, Oram MW (1997) Recognizing, understanding and reproducing actions. In: Jeannerod M, Grafman J (eds) Handbook of neuropsychology. Vol. 11: Action and cognition. Elsevier, Amsterdam.

Carr L, Iacoboni M, Dubeau MC, Mazziotta JC, Lenzi GL (2003) Neural mechanisms of empathy in humans: a relay from neural systems for imitation to limbic areas. Proc Natl Acad Sci USA 100: 5497–5502.

Changeux JP, Ricoeur P (1998) La nature et la règle. Odile Jacob, Paris.

Cochin S, Barthelemy C, Roux S, Martineau J (1999) Observation and execution of movement: similarities demonstrated by quantified electroencephalograpy. Eur J Neurosci 11: 1839– 1842.

Churchland, P.S. (1986), Neurophilosophy (Cambridge, MA: The MIT Press).

Churchland, P.S. & Ramachandran, V.S. (1993), 'Filling in: Why Dennett is wrong', in Dennett and His Critics: Demystifying Mind, ed. B. Dahlbom (Oxford: Blackwell Scientific Press).

Churchland, P.S., Ramachandran, V.S. & Sejnowski, T.J. (1994), 'A critique of pure vision', in Large- scale Neuronal Theories of the Brain, ed. C. Koch & J.L. Davis (Cambridge, MA: The MIT Press).

Crick, F. (1994), The Astonishing Hypothesis: The Scientific Search for the Soul (New York: Simon and Schuster).

Crick, F. (1996), 'Visual perception: rivalry and consciousness', Nature, 379.

Crick, F. & Koch, C. (1992), 'The problem of consciousness', Scientific American, 267.

Craig AD (2002) How do you feel? Interoception: the sense of the physiological condition of the body. Nature Rev Neurosci 3: 655–666.

Damasio, A (2003a) Looking for Spinoza. Harcourt Inc. Damasio A (2003b) Feeling of emotion and the self. Ann NY Acad Sci 1001: 253–261.

d'Aquili, Eugene. "Senses of Reality in Science and Religion." Zygon 17, no 4 (1982)

d'Aquili, Eugene. "The Biopsychological Determinants of Religious Ritual Behavior." Zygon 10, no. 1 (1975)

d'Aquili, Eugene. "The Myth-Ritual Complex: A Biogenetic Structural Analysis." Zygon 18, no. 3 (1983)

d'Aquili, Eugene, and Andrew Newberg. The Mystical Mind: Probing the Biology of Religious Experience. Minneapolis: Fortress Press, 1999.

Daly DD. 1958. Ictal affect. Am J Psychiatry.

Damasio, A. (1994) Descartes' Error: Emotion, Reason and the Human Brain. New York, Putnams.

Damasio, A. (1999) The Feeling of What Happens: Body, Emotion and the Making of Consciousness. London, Heinemann.

Darwin, C. (1859) On the Origin of Species by Means of Natural Selection. London, Murray.

Darwin, C. (1871) The Descent of Man and Selection in Relation to Sex. London, John Murray.

Darwin, C. (1872) The Expression of the Emotions in Man and Animals. London, John Murray; also published 1965, Chicago, University of Chicago Press.

Dawkins, M.S. (1987) Minding and mattering. In C. Blakemore and S. Greenfield (eds) Mindwaves. Oxford, Blackwell, 151-60.

Dawkins, R. (1976) The Selfish Gene. Oxford, Oxford University Press; a new edition, with additional material, was published in 1989.

Dawkins, R. (1986) The Blind Watchmaker. London, Longman.

Di Pellegrino G, Fadiga L, Fogassi L, Gallese V, Rizzolatti G (1992) Understanding motor events: A neurophysiological study. Exp Brain Res 91: 176–80.

Deikman, A.J. (2000) A functional approach to mysticism. Journal of Consciousness Studies 7(11-12), 75-91.

Delmonte, M.M. (1987) Personality and meditation. In M. West (ed.) The Psychology of Meditation. Oxford, Clarendon Press, 118-32.

Dennett, D.C. (1976) Are dreams experiences? Philosophical Review 73, 151-71; also reprinted in D.C. Dennett (1978) Brainstorms: Philosophical

Essays on Mind and Psychology. Harmondsworth, Penguin, 129-48.

Dennett, D.C. (1987) The Intentional Stance. Cambridge, MA, MIT Press.

Dennett, D.C. (1988) Quining qualia. In A.J. Marcel and E. Bisiach (eds) Consciousness in Contemporary Science. Oxford, Oxford University Press, 42-77.

Dennett, D.C. (1991) Consciousness Explained. Boston, MA, and London, Little, Brown and Co.

Dennett, D.C. (1995a) Darwin's Dangerous Idea. London, Penguin.

Dennett, D.C. (1995b) The unimagined preposterousness of zombies. Journal of Consciousness Studies 2(4), 322-6.

Dennett, D.C. (1995c) Cog: steps towards consciousness in robots. In T. Metzinger (ed.) Conscious Experience. Thorverton, Devon, Imprint Academic, 471-87.

Dennett, D.C. (1995d) The path not taken. Behavioral and Brain Sciences 18, 252-3; commentary on N. Block, On a confusion about a function of consciousness. Behavioral and Brain Sciences 18, 227.

Dennett, D.C. (1996a) Facing backwards on the problem of consciousness. Journal of Consciousness Studies 3(1), 4-6.

Dennett, D.C. (1996b) Kinds of Minds: Towards an Understanding of Consciousness. London, Weidenfeld & Nicolson.

Dennett, D.C. (1997) An exchange with Daniel Dennett. In J. Searle (ed.) The Mystery of Consciousness. New York, New York Review of Books, 115-19.

Dennett, D.C. (1998) The myth of double transduction. In S.R. Hameroff, A.W. Kaszniak and A. C. Scott (eds) Toward a Science of Consciousness: The Second Tucson Discussions and

Debates. Cambridge, MA, MIT Press, 97-107.

Dennett, D.C. (1998b) Brainchildren: Essays on Designing Minds. Cambridge, MA, MIT Press.

Dennett, D.C. (2001) The fantasy of first person science. Debate with D. Chalmers, Northwestern University, Evanston, IL, February 2001.

Dennett, D.C. (2003) Freedom Evolves. New York, Penguin.

Dennett, D.C. and Kinsbourne, M. (1992) Time and the observer: the where and when of consciousness in the brain. Behavioral and Brain Sciences 15, 183-247, including commentaries and authors' responses.

Dewhurst, Kenneth, and A. W. Beard. "Sudden Religious Conversions in Temporal Lobe Epilepsy." British Journal of Psychiatry 117 (1970)

Dewhurst K, Beard AW. Sudden religious conversions in temporal lobe epilepsy. 1970 Epilepsy Behav 2003

Devinsky O, Lai G. Spirituality and religion in epilepsy. Epilepsy Behav 2008.

Devinsky, O., Morrell, MJ, Vogt, BA. (1995) 'Contribution of anterior cingulate cortex to behavior', Brain, 118.

Eckhart Meister, Selected Writings

Fadiga L, Fogassi L, Pavesi G, Rizzolatti G (1995) Motor facilitation during action observation: a magnetic stimulation study. J Neurophysiol 73: 2608–2611.

Fogassi L, Gallese V, Fadiga L, Rizzolatti G (1998) Neurons responding to the sight of goal directed hand/arm actions in the parietal area PF (7b) of the macaque monkey. Soc Neurosci Abs 24:257.5.

Frith U, Frith CD (2003) Development and neurophysiology of mentalizing. Philos Trans R Soc Lond B Biol Sci 358: 459.

Frontera JG (1956) Some results obtained by electrical stimulation of the cortex of the island of Reil in the brain of the monkey (Macaca mulatta). J Comp Neurol 105: 365–394.

Farah, M.J. (1989), 'The neural basis of mental imagery', Trends in Neurosciences, 10.

Finlay BL, Darlington RB (1995) Linked regularities in the development and evolution of mammalian brains. Science 268.

Freud, S. "The Interpretation of Dreams", 1900

Freud, S. "Selected papers on hysteria and other psychoneuroses" Journal of Nervous and Mental Disease 1909.

Freud, S. "The Origin and Development of Psychoanalysis", 1910

Freud, S. "Psychopathology of everyday life", 1914

Freud, S. "Beyond the Pleasure Principle", 1920

Frith, C.D. & Dolan, R.J. (1997), 'Abnormal beliefs: Delusions and memory', Paper presented at the May, 1997, Harvard Conference on Memory and Belief.

Gay, Volney, ed. Neuroscience and Religion. Plymouth, UK: Lexington Books, 2009.

Gazzaniga, M. S. (1985). The social brain. New York: Basic Books.

Gazzaniga, M.S. (1993), 'Brain mechanisms and conscious experience', Ciba Foundation Symposium, 174.

Geschwind N. "Behavioural changes in temporal lobe epilepsy". Psychol Med. 1979.

Gellhorn, E., Kiely, W.F. "Mystical states of consciousness: neurophysiological and clinical aspects." J Nerv Ment Dis. 1972;154:399-405.

Gilbert SL, Dobyns WB, Lahn BT (2005) Genetic links between brain development and brain evolution. Nat Rev Genet 6.

Gray JA. The Psychology of Fear and Stress. 2nd ed. New York, NY: Cambridge University Press; 1988.

Gray JA. The Neuropsychology of Anxiety: An Enquiry into the Functions of the Septo Hippocampal System. 2nd ed. New York, NY: Oxford University Press; 2003.

Gloor, P. (1992), 'Amygdala and temporal lobe epilepsy', in The Amygdala: Neurobiological Aspects of

Emotion, Memory and Mental Dysfunction, ed J.P. Aggleton (New York: Wiley-Liss).

Greenspan, S. I. and S. G. Shanker (2004). The first idea: How symbols, language, and intelligence evolved from our early primate ancestors to modern humans. Cambridge, MA: Da Capo Press.

Grady, D. (1993), 'The vision thing: Mainly in the brain', Discover, June.

Graham DT. Prediction of fainting in blood donors. Circulation. 1961;23:901-906.

Grubb BP, Olshansky B. Syncope: Mechanisms and Management. 1st ed. New York, NY: Futura Publishing Company; 1998.

Gallagher HL, Frith CD (2003) Functional imaging of 'theory of mind'. Trends Cogn Sci 7: 77.

Gallese V, Fogassi L, Fadiga L, Rizzolatti G (2002) Action representation and the inferior parietal lobule. In: Prinz W, Hommel B (eds) Attention & Performance XIX. Common mechanisms in perception and action. Oxford University Press, Oxford.

Gallese V, Keysers C, Rizzolatti G (2004) A unifying view of the basis of social cognition. Trends Cogn Sci 8: 396–403.

Gangitano M, Mottaghy FM, Pascual-Leone A (2001) Phase specific modulation of cortical motor output during movement observation. NeuroReport 12: 1489–1492.

Gangitano M, Mottaghy FM, Pascual-Leone A (2004) Modulation of premotor mirror neuron activity during observation of unpredictable grasping movements. Eur J Neurosci 20: 2193– 2202.

Goldman AI, Sripada CS (2004) Simulationist models of face-based emotion recognition. Cognition 94: 193–213.

Grafton ST, Arbib MA, Fadiga L, Rizzolatti G (1996) Localization of grasp representations in humans by PET: 2. Observation compared with imagination. Exp Brain Res 112: 103–111.

Grèzes J, Costes N, Decety J (1998) Top-down effect of strategy on the perception of human biological motion: a PET investigation. Cogn Neuropsychol 15: 553–582.

Grèzes J, Armony JL, Rowe J, Passingham RE (2003) Activations related to "mirror" and "canonical" neurones in the human brain: an fMRI study. Neuroimage 18: 928–937.

Gross CG, Rocha-Miranda CE, Bender DB (1972) Visual properties of neurons in the inferotemporal cortex of the macaque. J Neurophysiol 35: 96–111.

Hari R, Forss N, Avikainen S, Kirveskari S, Salenius S, Rizzolatti G (1998) Activation of human primary motor cortex during action observation: a neuromagnetic study. Proc. Natl Acad Sci USA 95: 15061–15065.

Hall, Daniel, Keith Meador, and Harold Koenig. "Measuring Religiousness in Health Research: Review and Critique." Journal of Religion and Health 47, no. 2 (2008)

Harris, Sam, Jonas Kaplan, Ashley Curiel, Susan Bookheimer, Marco Iacoboni, and Mark Cohen. "The Neural Correlates of Religious and Nonreligious Belief." PLoS One 4, no. 10 (October 1, 2009)

Halgren, E. (1992), 'Emotional neurophysiology of the amygdala within the context of human cognition', in The Amygdala: Neurobiological Aspects of Emotion, Memory and Mental Dysfunction, ed J.P. Aggleton (New York: Wiley-Liss).

Halligan PW, Fink GR, Marshal JC, Vallar G. 2003. Spatial cognition: evidence from visual neglect. Trends Cogn Sci.

Handbook of Emotions, Edited by Michael Lewis, Jeannette M. Haviland-Jones, and Lisa Feldman Barrett, The Guilford Press; 3rd edition (2010).

Haggard, P., Clark, S. and Kalogeras,]. (2002) Voluntary action and conscious awareness, Nature Neuroscience 5, 382-5. Haggard, P., Newman, C. and Magno, E. (1999) On the perceived time of voluntary actions. British Journal of Psychology 90, 291-303.

Hameroff, S.R. and Penrose, R. (1996) Conscious events as orchestrated space-time selections. Journal of Consciousness Studies 3(1), 36-53; also reprinted in J. Shear (ed.) (1997) Explaining Consciousness-The Hard Problem. Cambridge, MA, MIT Press, 177-95.

Hardcastle, V.G. (2000) How to understand theN in NCC. InT. Metzinger (ed.) Neural Correlates of Consciousness. Cambridge, MA, MIT Press, 259-64.

Harding, D.E. (1961) On Having no Head: Zen and the Re-Discovery of the Obvious. London, Buddhist Society.

Hardy, A. (1979) The Spiritual Nature of Man: A Study of Contemporary Religious Experience. Oxford, Clarendon Press.

Hamad, S. (1990) The symbol grounding problem. Physica D 42, 335-46.

Hamad, S. (2001) No easy way out. The Sciences 41(2), 36-42.

Harre, R. and Gillett, G. (1994) The Discursive Mind. Thousand Oaks, CA, Sage.

Haugeland, J. (ed.) (1997) Mind Design II: Philosophy, Psychology, Artificial Intelligence. Cambridge, MA, MIT Press.

Hauser, M.D. (2000) Wild Minds: What Animals Really Think. New York, Henry Holt and Co.; London, Penguin.

Hearne, K. (1990) The Dream Machine. Northants, Aquarian.

Hebb, D.O. (1949) The Organization of Behavior. New York, Wiley.

Helmholtz, H.L.F. von (1856-67) Treatise on Physiological Optics.

Heyes, C.M. (1998) Theory of mind in nonhuman primates. Behavioral and Brain Sciences 21, 101-48; with commentaries.

Heyes, C.M. and Galef, B.G. (eds) (1996) Social Learning in Animals: The

Roots of Culture. San Diego, CA, Academic Press.

Hilgard, E.R. (1986) Divided Consciousness: Multiple Controls in Human Thought and Action. New York, Wiley.

Hodgson, R. (1891) A case of double consciousness. Proceedings of the Society for Psychical Research 7, 221-58.

Hofstadter, D.R. (1979) Code!, Escher, Bach: An Eternal Golden Braid. London, Penguin.

Hofstadter, D.R. and Dennett, D.C. (eds) (1981) The Mind's I: Fantasies and Reflections on Self and Soul. London, Penguin.

Holland, J. (ed.) (2001) Ecstasy: The Complete Guide: A Comprehensive Look at the Risks and Benefits of MDMA. Rochester, VT, Park Street Press.

Holmes, D.S. (1987) The influence of meditation versus rest on physiological arousal. In M. West (ed.) The Psychology of Meditation. Oxford, Clarendon Press, 81-103.

Holt, J. (1999) Blindsight in debates about qualia. Journal of Consciousness Studies 6(5), 54-71.

Horgan, J. (1994), 'Can science explain consciousness?', Scientific American, 271.

Holloway RL (1996) Evolution of the human brain. In: Lock A, Peters CR (eds) Handbook of human symbolic evolution. Oxford University Press, Oxford

Iacoboni M, Woods RP, Brass M, Bekkering H, Mazziotta JC, Rizzolatti G (1999) Cortical mechanisms of human imitation. Science 286: 2526–2528.

Iacoboni M, Koski LM, Brass M, Bekkering H, Woods RP, Dubeau MC,

Mazziotta JC, Rizzolatti G (2001) Reafferent copies of imitated actions in the right superior temporal cortex. Proc Natl Acad Sci USA 98: 13995–13999.

Jeannerod M (1988) The neural and behavioural organization of goal-directed movements. Clarendon Press, Oxford.

Johnson-Frey SH, Maloof FR, Newman-Norlund R, Farrer C, Inati S, Grafton ST (2003) Actions or hand-objects interactions? Human inferior frontal cortex and action observation. Neuron 39: 1053–1058.

Jackson, F. (1982) Epiphenomenal qualia. Philosophical Quarterly 32, 127-36.

James, W. (1890) The Principles of Psychology (2 volumes). London, Macmillan.

James, W. (1902) The Varieties of Religious Experience: A Study in

Human Nature. New York and London, Longmans, Green and Co.

Jansen, K. (2001) Ketamine: Dreams and Realities. Sarasota, FL, Multidisciplinary Association for Psychedelic Studies.

Jay, M. (ed.) (1999) Artificial Paradises: A Drugs Reader. London, Penguin.

Jaynes, J. (1976) The Origin of Consciousness in the Breakdown of the Bicameral Mind. New York, Houghton Mifflin.

Johnson, M.K. and Raye, C.L. (1981) Reality monitoring. Psychological Review 88, 67-85.

Julien, R.M. (2001) A Primer of Drug Action: A Concise, Nontechnical Guide to the Actions, Uses, and Side Effects of Psychoactive Drugs (revised edn). New York, Henry Holt.

Kaada BR, Pribram KH, Epstein JA (1949) Respiratory and vascular responses in monkeys from temporal pole, insula, orbital surface and cingulate gyrus: a preliminary report. J Neurophysiol 12: 347–356.

Kohler E, Keysers C, Umiltà MA, Fogassi L, Gallese V, Rizzolatti G (2002). Hearing sounds, understanding actions: action Rrepresentation in mirror neurons. Science 297: 846–848.

Koski L, Wohlschlager A, Bekkering H, Woods RP, Dubeau MC (2002) Modulation of motor and premotor activity during imitation of target-directed actions. Cereb Cortex 12: 847–855.

Koski L, Iacoboni M, Dubeau MC, Woods RP, Mazziotta JC (2003) Modulation of cortical activity during different imitative behaviors. J Neurophysiol 89: 460–471.

Krolak-Salmon P, Henaff MA, Isnard J, Tallon-Baudry C, Guenot M, Vighetto A, Bertrand O, Mauguiere F (2003) An attention modulated response to disgust in human ventral anterior insula. Ann Neurol 53: 446–453.

Kandel, E. R. In Search of Memory: The Emergence of a New Science of Mind, W. W. Norton & Company (2007).

Kandel E. R. Schwartz JH, Jessel TM. Principles of neural sciences. New York; McGraw Hill, 2000.

Kanizsa, G. (1979), Organization In Vision (New York: Praeger).

Kaloupek DG, Scott JR, Khatami V. Assessment of coping strategies associated with syncope in blood donors. J Psychosom Res. 1985;29:207-214.

Kanwisher, N. (2001) Neural events and perceptual awareness. Cognition 79, 89-113; also reprinted inS. Dehaene (ed.) The Cognitive Neuroscience of Consciousness. Cambridge, MA, MIT Press, 89-113.

Kapleau, Roshi P. (1980) The Three Pillars of Zen: Teaching, Practice, and Enlightenment (revised edn). New York, Doubleday.

Karn, K. and Hayhoe, M. (2000) Memory representations guide targeting eye movements in a natural task. Visual Cognition 7, 673-703.

Kasamatsu, A. and Hirai, T. (1966) An electroencephalographic study on the Zen meditation (zazen). Folia Psychiatrica et Neurologica Japonica 20, 315-36.

Kaiserman-Abramof, I. R., Graybiel, A. M., & Nauta, W. J. (1980). The thalamic projection to cortical area 17 in a congenitally anophthalmic mouse strain. Neuroscience, 5, 41–52.

Kanold, P. O., Kara, P., Reid, R. C., & Shatz, C. J. (2003). Role of subplate neurons in functional maturation of visual cortical columns. Science, 301, 521–525.

Kennedy, H., & Dehay, C. (1988). Functional implications of the anatomical organization of the callosal projections of visual areas V1 and V2 in the macaque monkey. Behav. Brain Res., 29, 225–236.

Kennedy, H., & Dehay, C. (1993). Cortical specifi cation of mice and men. Cereb. Cortex, 3, 171–186.

Koketsu, D., Mikami, A., Miyamoto, Y., & Hisatsune, T. (2003). Nonrenewal of neurons in the cerebral neocortex of adult macaque monkeys. J. Neurosci., 23, 937–942.

Komuro, H., & Rakic, P. (1992). Selective role of N-type calcium channels in neuronal migration. Science, 257, 806–809.

Komuro, H., & Rakic, P. (1993). Modulation of neuronal migration by NMDA receptors. Science, 260, 95–97.

Komuro, H., & Rakic, P. (1996). Intracellular Ca2+ fl uctuations modulate the rate of neuronal migration. Neuron, 17, 275–285.

Kornack, D. R., & Rakic, P. (1995). Radial and horizontal deployment of clonally related cells in the primate neocortex: Relation- ship to distinct mitotic lineages. Neuron, 15, 311–321.

Kornack, D. R., & Rakic, P. (1999). Continuation of neurogenesis in the hippocampus of the adult macaque monkey. Proc. Natl. Acad. Sci. USA, 96, 5768–5773.

Kornack, D. R., & Rakic, P. (2001a). Cell proliferation without neurogenesis in adult primate neocortex. Science, 294, 2127–2130.

Kornack, D. R., & Rakic, P. (2001b). The generation, migration, and differentiation of olfactory neurons in the adult primate brain. Proc. Natl. Acad. Sci. USA, 98, 4752–4757.

Kostovic, I., & Molliver, D. E. (1974). A new interpretation of the laminar development of cerebral cortex: Synaptogenesis in different layers of neopalium in the human fetus. Anat. Rec., 178, 395.

Kostovic, I., & Rakic, P. (1980). Cytology and time of origin of interstitial neurons in the white matter in infant and adult human and monkey telencephalon. J. Neurocytol., 9, 219–242.

Kostovic, I., & Rakic, P. (1984). Development of prestriate visual projections in the monkey and human fetal cerebrum revealed by transient cholinesterase staining. J. Neurosci., 4, 25–42.

Kennett, J. (1972) Selling Water by the River. London, Allen & Unwin; also published by New York, Vintage.

Kentridge, R.W. and Heywood, C.A. (1999) The status of blindsight. Journal of Consciousness Studies 6(5), 3-11.

Kihlstrom, J.F. (1996) Perception without awareness of what is perceived, learning without awareness of what is learned. In M. Velmans (ed.) The Science of Consciousness. London, Routledge, 23-46.

Kluver, H. (1926) Mescal visions and eidetic vision. American Journal of Psychology 37, 502-15.

Kollerstrom, N. (1999) The path of Halley's comet, and Newton's late apprehension of the law of gravity. Annals of Science 56, 331-56.

Kosslyn, S.M. (1980) Image and Mind. Cambridge, MA, Harvard University Press.

Kosslyn, S.M. (1988) Aspects of a cognitive neuroscience of mental imagery. Science 240, 1621-6.

Kinsbourne, M. (1995), 'The intralaminar thalamic nucleii', Consciousness and Cognition, 4.

Kjaer, Troels, Camilla Bertelsen, Paola Piccini, David Brooks, Jorgen Alving, and Hans Lou. "Increased Dopamine Tone during Meditation- Induced Change of Consciousness." Cognitive Brain Research 13, no. 2 (April 2002)

Kölmel HW. 1985. Complex visual hallucinations in the hemianopic field. J Neurol Neurosurg Psychiatry.

Koenig, Harold. "Research on Religion, Spirituality, and Mental Health: A Review." Canadian Journal of Psychiatry 54, no. 5 (May 2009)

Koenig, Harold, ed. Handbook of Religion and Mental Health. San Diego, CA: Academic Press, 1998

Kraepelin E. Psychiatry: A Textbook for Students and Physicians. New York, NY: Science History Publications; 1990.

Lauglin, Charles, John McManus, and Eugene d'Aquili. Brain, Symbol, and

Experience. 2nd ed. New York: Columbia University Press, 1992

Lakoff, G. and M. Johnson (1999). Philosophy in the flesh. Basic Books: New York.

LeDoux, J. E. (1996). The emotional brain. New York: Simon & Schuster.

LeDoux, J.E. (1992), 'Emotion and the amygdala', in The Amygdala: Neurobiological Aspects of Emo- tion, Memory and Mental Dysfunction, ed J.P. Aggleton (New York: Wiley-Liss).

Levin, D.T. and Simons, D.J. (1997) Failure to detect changes to attended objects in motion pictures. Psychonomic Bulletin and Review 4, 501-6.

Levine,J. (1983) Materialism and qualia: the explanatory gap. Pacific Philosophical Quarterly 64, 354-61.

Levine,J. (2001) Purple Haze: The Puzzle of Consciousness. New York, Oxford University Press. Levine, S.

(1979) A Gradual Awakening. New York, Doubleday.

Levinson, B.W. (1965) States of awareness during general anaesthesia. British Journal of Anaesthesia 37, 544-6.

Lewicki, P., Czyzewska, M. and Hoffman, H. (1987) Unconscious acquisition of complex procedural knowledge. Journal of Experimental Psychology: Learning, Memory and Cognition 13, 523-30.

Lewicki, P., Hill, T. and Bizot, E. (1988) Acquisition of procedural knowledge about a pattern of stimuli that cannot be articulated. Cognitive Psychology 20, 24-37.

Lewicki, P., Hill, T. and Czyzewska, M. (1992) Nonconscious acquisition of information. American Psychologist 47, 796-801.

Manthey S, Schubotz RI, von Cramon DY (2003). Premotor cortex in observing erroneous action: an fMRI study. Brain Res Cogn Brain Res 15: 296–307.

Mesulam MM, Mufson EJ (1982) Insula of the old world monkey. III: Efferent cortical output and comments on function. J Comp Neurol 212: 38–52.

Naskar, Abhijit. "What is Mind?", 2016

Naskar, Abhijit. "In Search of Divinity: Journey to The Kingdom of Conscience", 2016

Naskar, Abhijit. "Love, God & Neurons: Memoir of A Scientist who found himself by getting lost", 2016

Naskar, Abhijit. "Neurons of Jesus: Mind of A Teacher, Spouse & Thinker", 2017

Naskar, Abhijit. "Rowdy Buddha: The First Sapiens", 2017

Naskar, Abhijit. "The Education Decree", 2017

Naskar, Abhijit. "Principia Humanitas", 2017

Naskar, Abhijit. "Either Civilized or Phobic: A Treatise on Homosexuality", 2017

Naskar, Abhijit. "We Are All Black: A Treatise on Racism", 2017

Naskar, Abhijit. "Wise Mating: A Treatise on Monogamy", 2017

Naskar, Abhijit. "Illusion of Religion: A Treatise on Religious Fundamentalism", 2017

Naskar, Abhijit. "I Am The Thread: My Mission", 2017

Naskar, Abhijit. "Morality Absolute", 2017

Naskar, Abhijit. "Time to Save Medicine", 2018

Newberg, Andrew, and Jeremy Iversen. "The Neural Basis of the Complex Mental Task of Meditation:

Neurotransmitter and Neurochemical Considerations." Medical Hypotheses 61, no. 2 (2003).

Newberg, Andrew. "How God Changes Your Brain: An Introduction to Jewish Neurotheology", CCAR Journal: The Reform Jewish Quarterly, Winter 2016.

Newberg, Andrew, and Stephanie Newberg. "A Neuropsychological Perspective on Spiritual Development." In Handbook of Spiritual Development in Childhood and Adolescence, edited by Eugene Roehlkepartain, Pamela King, Linda Wagener, and Peter Benson. London: Sage Publications, Inc., 2005

Newberg, Andrew. "The Neurotheology Link An Intersection Between Spirituality and Health", Alternative and Complimentary Therapies, Vol 21 No 1, February 2015.

Newberg, Andrew, Nancy Wintering, Dharma Khalsa, Hannah Roggenkamp, and Mark Waldman. "Meditation Effects on Cognitive Function and Cerebral Blood Flow in Subjects with Memory Loss: A Preliminary Study." Journal of Alzheimer's Disease 20, no. 2 (2010)

Nash, M. (1995), 'Glimpses of the mind', Time.

Nesse RM. Proximate and evolutionary studies of anxiety, stress and depression: synergy at the interface. Neurosci Biobehav Rev. 1999;23:895-903.

Nishitani N, Hari R (2000) Temporal dynamics of cortical representation for action. Proc Natl Acad Sci USA 97: 913–918.

Nishitani N, Hari R (2002) Viewing lip forms: cortical dynamics. Neuron 36: 1211–1220.

O'Hara, K. and Scutt, T. (1996) There is no hard problem of consciousness. Journal of Consciousness Studies 3(4), 290-302, reprinted in J. Shear (ed.) (1997) Explaining Consciousness. Cambridge, MA, MIT Press, 69-82.

O'Regan, J.K. (1992) Solving the "real" mysteries of visual perception: the world as an outside memory. Canadian Journal of Psychology 46, 461-88.

O'Regan, J.K. and Noe, A. (2001) A sensorimotor account of vision and visual consciousness. Behavioral and Brain Sciences 24(5), 883-917.

O'Regan, J.K., Rensink, R.A. and Clark,].]. (1999) Change-blindness as a result of "mudsplashes." Nature 398, 34.

Ornstein, R.E. (1977) The Psychology of Consciousness (2nd edn). New York, Harcourt.

Ornstein, R.E. (1986) The Psychology of Consciousness (3rd edn). New York, Pehguin.

Ornstein, R.E. (1992) The Evolution of Consciousness. New York, Touchstone.

Penfield W, Faulk ME (1955) The insula: further observations on its function. Brain 78: 445– 470.

Penrose, R. (1994), Shadows of the Mind (Oxford: Oxford University Press).

Penrose, R. (1989), The Emperor's New Mind: Concerning Computers, Minds and The Laws of Physics (Oxford: Oxford University Press).

Persinger, "'I would kill in God's name' role of sex, weekly church attendance, report of a religious experience and limbic lability" Perceptual and Motor Skills 1997.

Persinger "Experimental simulation of the God experience" Neurotheology 2003.

Persinger, M. A. (1993b). Personality changes following brain injury as a grief response to the loss of sense of self: Phenomenological themes as indices of local lability and neurocognitive restructuring as psycho- therapy. Psychological Reports, 72

Persinger, Corradini, Clement, Keaney, et al "Neurotheology and its convergence with neuroquantology" NeuroQuantology 2010.

Persinger, Koren and St-Pierre "The electromagnetic induction of mystical and altered states within the laboratory" Journal of Consciousness Exploration and Research 2010.

Persinger "Case report: A prototypical spontaneous 'sensed presence' of a sentient being and concomitant electroencephalographic activity in the clinical laboratory" Neurocase 2008.

Persinger and Saroka "Potential production of Hughlings Jackson's "parasitic consciousness" by physiologically-patterned weak transcerebral magnetic fields: QEEG and source localization" Epilepsy & Behavior 28 (2013).

Persinger. "The neuropsychiatry of paranormal experiences". J Neuropsychiatry Clin Neurosci 2001.

Persinger. "Neuropsychological bases of god beliefs", New York: Praeger, 1987

Persinger. "Temporal lobe epileptic signs and correlative behaviors displayed by normal populations", Journal of General Psychology, 1986

Persinger "Experimental Facilitation of the Sensed Presence: Possible Intercalation between the Hemispheres Induced by Complex Magnetic Fields"

Journal of Nervous and Mental Disease 2002.

Palmer J. 1978. The out-of-body experience: a psychological theory. Parapsychol Rev.

Page AC. Blood-injury phobia. Clinical Psychology Review. 1994;14:443-461.

Perry BD, Pollard R. Homeostasis, stress, trauma, and adaptation. A neurodevelopmental view of childhood trauma. Child Adolesc Psychiatr Clin N Am. 1998;7:33.

Paré, D. & Llinás, R. (1995), 'Conscious and preconscious processes as seen from the standpoint of sleep-waking cycle neurophysiology', Neuropsychologia, 33.

P. S. de Laplace. Essai Philosophique sur les Probabilites [1814], in Academy des Sciences, Oeuvres Complotes de Laplace, Vol. 7, Gauthier-Villars, Paris (1886).

Perrett DI, Harries MH, Bevan R, Thomas S, Benson PJ, Mistlin AJ, Chitty AJ, Hietanen JK, Ortega JE (1989) Frameworks of analysis for the neural representation of animate objects and actions. J Exp Bio 146: 87–113.

Phillips ML, Young AW, Senior C, Brammer M, Andrew C, Calder AJ, Bullmore ET, Perrett DI, Rowland D, Williams SC, Gray JA, David AS (1997) A specific neural substrate for perceiving facial expressions of disgust. Nature 389: 495–498.

Phillips ML, Young AW, Scott SK, Calder AJ, Andrew C, Giampietro V, Williams SC, Bullmore ET, Brammer M, Gray JA (1998) Neural responses to facial and vocal expressions of fear and disgust. Proc R Soc Lond B Biol Sci 265: 1809–1817.

Puce A, Perrett D (2003) Electrophysiological and brain imaging of biological motion.

Philosoph Trans Royal Soc Lond, Series B, 358: 435–445.

Ramachandran VS. Behavioral and magnetoencephalographic correlates of plasticity in the adult human brain. Proc Natl Acad Sci USA 1993; 90: 10413–20.

Ramachandran VS. Phantom limbs, neglect syndromes, repressed memories, and Freudian psychology. Int Rev Neurobiol 1994; 37: 291–333.

Ramachandran VS. Plasticity and functional recovery in neurology. Clin Med 2005; 5: 368–73.

Ramachandran VS, Hirstein W. The perception of phantom limbs. The D. O. Hebb lecture. Brain 1998; 121: 1603–30.

Ramachandran VS, McGeoch PD, Williams L, Arcilla G. Rapid relief of thalamic pain syndrome induced by vestibular caloric stimulation. Neurocase 2007; 13: 185–8.

Ramachandran VS, Rogers-Ramachandran D, Cobb S. Touching the phantom limb. Nature 1995; 377: 489–90.

Ramachandran VS, Rogers-Ramachandran D. Phantom limbs and neural plasticity. Arch Neurol 2000; 57: 317–20.

Ramachandran VS, Rogers-Ramachandran D. It's all done with mirrors. Sci Am Mind 2007; 18: 16–9.

Ramachandran VS, Rogers-Ramachandran D. Sensations referred to a patient's phantom arm from another subjects intact arm: perceptual correlates of mirror neurons. Med Hypotheses 2008; 70: 1233–4.

Ramachandran VS, Rogers-Ramachandran D, Stewart M. Perceptual correlates of massive cortical reorganization. Science 1992; 258: 1159–60.

Rizzolatti G, Craighero L (2004) The mirror-neuron system. Annu Rev Neurosci 27: 169–192.

Rizzolatti G, Scandolara C, Matelli M, Gentilucci M (1981) Afferent properties of periarcuate neurons in macaque monkeys. I. Somatosensory responses. Behav Brain Res 2: 125–146.

Rizzolatti G, Fadiga L, Matelli M, Bettinardi V, Paulesu E, Perani D, Fazio F (1996) Localization of grasp representation in humans by PET: 1. Observation versus execution. Exp Brain Res 111: 246–252.

Rizzolatti G, Fogassi L, Gallese V (2001) Neurophysiological mechanisms underlying the understanding and imitation of action. Nature Rev Neurosci 2:661–670.

Rock I, Victor J. Vision and touch: an experimentally created conflict between the two senses. Science 1964; 143: 594–6.

Rose'n B, Lundborg G. Training with a mirror in rehabilitation of the hand. Scand J Plast Reconstr Surg Hand Surg 2005; 39: 104–8.

Royet JP, Plailly J, Delon-Martin C, Kareken DA, Segebarth C (2003) fMRI of emotional responses to odors: influence of hedonic valence and judgment, handedness, and gender. Neuroimage 20: 713–728.

Rozin R Haidt J and McCauley CR (2000) Disgust. In: Lewis M, Haviland-Jones JM (eds) Handbook of Emotion. 2nd Edition. Guilford Press, New York, pp 637–653.

Saxe R, Carey S, Kanwisher N (2004) Understanding other minds: linking developmental psychology and functional neuroimaging. Annu Rev Psychol 55: 87–124.

Schienle A, Stark R, Walter B, Blecker C, Ott U, Kirsch P, Sammer G, Vaitl D (2002) The insula is not specifically involved in disgust processing: an fMRI study. Neuroreport 13: 2023–2026.

Showers MJC, Lauer EW (1961) Somatovisceral motor patterns in the insula. J Comp Neurol 117: 107–115.

Singer T, Seymour B, O'Doherty J, Kaube H, Dolan RJ, Frith CD (2004) Empathy for pain involves the affective but not the sensory components of pain. Science 303: 1157–1162.

Small DM, Gregory MD, Mak YE, Gitelman D, Mesulam MM, Parrish T (2003) Dissociation of neural representation of intensity and affective valuation in human gustation Neuron 39: 701–711.

Smith A (1759) The theory of moral sentiments (ed. 1976). Clarendon Press, Oxford.

Sprengelmeyer R, Rausch M, Eysel UT, Przuntek H (1998) Neural structures associated with recognition of facial expressions of basic emotions Proc R Soc Lond B Biol Sci 265: 1927–1931.

Strafella AP, Paus T (2000) Modulation of cortical excitability during action observation: a transcranial magnetic stimulation study. NeuroReport 11: 2289–2292.

Tanaka K (1996) Inferotemporal cortex and object vision. Ann Rev Neurosci. 19: 109–140.

Tomasello M, Call J (1997) Primate cognition. Oxford University Press, Oxford.

Tremblay C, Robert M, Pascual-Leone A, Lepore F, Nguyen DK, Carmant L, Bouthillier A, Theoret H (2004) Action observation and execution: intracranial recordings in a human subject. Neurology. 63: 937–938.

Umilta MA, Kohler E, Gallese V, Fogassi L, Fadiga L, Keysers C, Rizzolatti G (2001) "I know what you are doing": a neurophysiological study. Neuron 32: 91–101.

Visalberghi E, Fragaszy D. (2002). Do monkeys ape? Ten years after. In: Dautenhahn K, Nehaniv C (eds) Imitation in animals and artifacts. MIT Press, Boston. Pp. 471–500

Wicker B, Keysers C, Plailly J, Royet JP, Gallese V, Rizzolatti G (2003) Both of us disgusted in my insula: the common neural basis of seeing and feeling disgust. Neuron 40: 655–664.

Yokochi H, Tanaka M, Kumashiro M, Iriki A (2003) Inferior parietal somatosensory neurons coding face-hand coordination in Japanese macaques. Somatosens Mot Res 20 : 115–125.

Zald DH, Pardo JV (2000) Functional neuroimaging of the olfactory system in humans. Int J Psychophysiol 36: 165–181.

Zald DH, Donndelinger MJ, Pardo JV (1998) Elucidating dynamic brain interactions with across-subjects correlational analyses of positron emission tomographic data: the functional connectivity of the amygdala and orbitofrontal cortex during olfactory tasks. J Cereb Blood Flow Metab 18: 896–905.

137

139

www.ingramcontent.com/pod-product-compliance
Lightning Source LLC
Chambersburg PA
CBHW051454250726
48655CB00001B/412